ULTIMATE
QUESTIONS & ANSWERS
ANIMALS
AND NATURE

AUTUMN PUBLISHING

CONTENTS:

WHAT IS AN ECOSYSTEM?

Mosquito
Dragonfly
Frog
Duck
Duckling
Pond Skater
Water Lily
Duck potato
Frog eggs
Fish
Leech
Tadpole
Water Snail
Water beetle
Newt
Water Scorpion

An ecosystem is an environment where plants, animals, and other living organisms, as well as nonliving things, such as water, rocks, and soil, interact with each other to form a unique community.

An ecosystem is interdependent.

Big ?

WHAT ARE THE DIFFERENT TYPES OF ECOSYSTEMS?

There are two main types of ecosystems: Ecosystems on land, called terrestrial ecosystems, which include forests, grasslands, and deserts, and ecosystems in water, called aquatic ecosystems, such as lakes, rivers, and oceans. Ecosystems can be small, medium, or large. The world's oceans make up a large ecosystem, while a tide pool—a pool of ocean water left behind when the tide goes out—is an example of a small ecosystem. Ecosystems are often connected in a larger biome. Biomes are areas on the planet that share similar things, such as climate, landscape, and certain types of plants and animals.

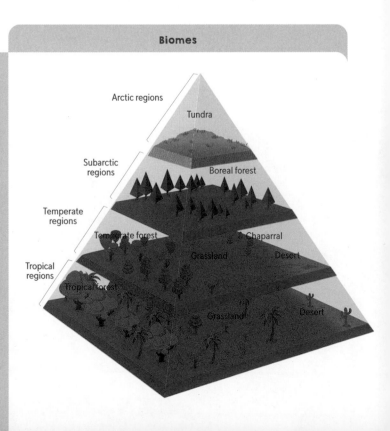

Biomes

Arctic regions
Tundra
Subarctic regions
Boreal forest
Temperate regions
Temperate forest
Chaparral
Grassland
Desert
Tropical regions
Tropical forest
Grassland
Desert

WHAT IS A HUMAN ECOSYSTEM?

An ecosystem that is made up of people, plants, animals, and other living things that interact and influence the physical environment. A farm is an example of a human ecosystem, because humans, animals, birds, fields, fences, roads, and buildings are all connected, influenced, and controlled by humans.

WHICH IS THE MOST DIVERSE ECOSYSTEM IN THE WORLD?

The huge Coral Triangle in Southeast Asia. It is a marine area located in the western Pacific Ocean. The ecosystem has 600 species of reef-building coral, six of the world's seven marine turtle species, and more than 2,000 species of reef fish!

Coral Triangle, Pacific Ocean

WHAT ARE THE THREATS TO ECOSYSTEMS?

For thousands of years, people have interacted with ecosystems. But ever-growing human populations threaten to destroy many ecosystems. Large areas of land have been cleared for farmland, housing, and industry. Removing and adding elements can cause an ecosystem to change in size and shape, affecting the way it functions. Human activity threatens ecosystems to the point where many may eventually collapse and disappear.

A natural ecosystem threatened by human waste

ARE ECOSYSTEMS WITHIN A BIOME ALWAYS SIMILAR?

No. Within the desert biome, for instance, the hot Sahara Desert is very different from the cold Gobi Desert in Mongolia and China.

CAN AN ECOSYSTEM RECOVER FROM DECLINE?

Yes, if conditions improve.

WHAT IS HUMAN ECOLOGY?

The study of the relationship between humans and their natural, social, and built environments.

WHAT IS A RAINFOREST?

Tropical rainforests occur in areas that are warm and wet, where rainfall is very high. These forests make up Earth's oldest living ecosystem—some have survived for at least 70 million years! Incredibly diverse and complex, tropical rainforests are home to half of the world's plant and animal species. The world's main tropical rainforests are in South and Central America, West and Central Africa, Southeast Asia, and north Australia.

WHAT ARE THE PARTS OF A RAINFOREST?

At the top of the tallest trees live birds, bats, gliders, and butterflies. Below the top is the canopy, a very deep, dense layer of vegetation that blocks wind, rainfall, and sunlight, creating a humid, still, and dark environment. Most of the forest's animals live in the canopy. Several yards below the canopy is the understory, a layer of shrubs that is darker and even more humid. It is home to some of the most familiar and endangered rainforest species. The forest floor is comparably empty.

Rapid-FIRE ?

WHO ARE THE YANOMAMI?

They are native people who live in the Amazon rainforest on the border between Venezuela and Brazil.

DOES RAIN REACH THE FOREST FLOOR?

The vegetation is so dense that it can take a raindrop 10 minutes to fall from the top of the forest to the floor!

HOW LONG CAN TREES LIVE FOR IN A RAINFOREST?

The Brazil nut tree can live up to 1,000 years in an undisturbed rainforest habitat!

Brazil nut tree

Amazon rainforest, South America

WHAT IS THE WORLD'S LARGEST TROPICAL RAINFOREST?

The Amazon in South America.

The tallest trees rise high above the forest canopy.

The dense canopy of a rainforest

Big? ARE RAINFORESTS IMPORTANT?

Yes, rainforests are vital. The tall evergreen trees help preserve our planet's atmosphere by absorbing carbon dioxide and releasing huge quantities of water vapor and oxygen, both essential to life. Rainforests regulate Earth's climate by reducing the impact of greenhouse gases and absorbing solar radiation. They store a considerable amount of the world's fresh water and help maintain the water cycle. Rainforests provide human beings with wood, spices, fruit, medicinal plants, and much more.

Logging

ARE RAINFORESTS IN DANGER?

Yes. The biggest cause of forest destruction is deforestation by humans. Huge areas of forests are burned down so that the land can be used for producing crops or for grazing domesticated animals. Logging companies cut rainforests down for lumber, and massive hydroelectric power projects create dams which flood acres of forest land.

WHAT IS A WOODLAND?

A woodland is an area mostly covered by trees that overlap, but the canopy is not very dense so sunlight filters through. Small shrubs and vegetation grow under the trees. The animals are smaller in size, and there are fewer predators. Woodlands can act as bridges between ecosystems such as grasslands, true forests, and deserts. True forests are larger and have denser foliage and closed canopies.

An evergreen forest

WHAT DO WE GET FROM TEMPERATE FORESTS?

Mostly lumber. When burned slowly, certain kinds of wood create charcoal. In the past, woodland animals, such as wild boar and deer, were used for food and for their skins (hides). Many edible fungi, including chanterelles and truffles, grow in temperate forests, while brambles and wild strawberries have tasty fruit.

Lumber

Rapid-FIRE?

HOW LONG CAN TREES LIVE?

Oaks can live between 200 and 400 years.

Oak tree

Hibernating chipmunk

WHAT TREE IS THE NOISIEST?

The aspen. Its leaves rustle against each other in the slightest breeze.

WHY DO TEMPERATE FORESTS BECOME QUIETER IN WINTER?

Because some birds migrate and smaller animals hibernate (go into a deep sleep).

HOW IS LUMBER HARVESTED FROM TEMPERATE FORESTS?

Many forests are not natural, but have been managed for centuries to provide wood. This involves removing only a portion of the tree at a time, which lets the forest regenerate. One such system is coppicing, in which the stems of a tree are cut to the ground from time to time. They resprout from the base to provide another crop of branches a few years later.

Coppiced woodland

DO FLOWERS GROW IN WOODLANDS?

Woodland flowers appear in spring; by developing early in the year they receive enough sunlight to grow before the tree foliage blocks out the sun. Many woodland insects help pollinate flowers.

Wild bluebells

Big? WHAT KIND OF LIFE THRIVES IN TEMPERATE WOODLANDS?

Eurasian bullfinch

Snail

Fallow deer

Hedgehog

The world's temperate regions lie between the tropics and the poles and have a variety of weathers and seasons. They have two types of woodlands. Deciduous woodlands are made up of trees that lose their leaves by winter. Evergreen woodland trees keep their leaves year-round. The most common trees in deciduous forests are oak, beech, maple, and birch. Common evergreen trees are conifers, such as pine, fir, and spruce. Fallow deer, badgers, foxes, weasels, moles, squirrels, mice, and voles live in temperate woodlands. The leaf litter beneath the trees is home to creatures including spiders, beetles, woodlice, worms, millipedes, snails, and ants. The trees themselves are a haven for many insects, birds, and small mammals.

WHAT IS A WETLAND?

Wetlands are areas that are either covered or saturated with water. They are found near oceans, rivers, estuaries (where a river meets the ocean), lakes, and marshes. There are different types of wetlands, that come in many shapes and forms including mangroves, mudflats, mires, ponds, fens, deltas, coral reefs, billabongs, lagoons, shallow seas, bogs, and floodplains.

HOW DO WATER PLANTS STAY AFLOAT?

Some water plants' tissues can fill up with air, making their stems and leaves buoyant. Others, such as water lilies, have flat, rounded leaves that sit boatlike on the water's surface. Some have waxy leaves, which repel the water, or leaves with up-curved rims that prevent water from washing over them.

Boatlike leaves of water lilies

Big? WHY ARE WETLANDS SO IMPORTANT?

During heavy rains, wetlands act like giant sponges or reservoirs, absorbing excess water and limiting the effects of flooding. Wetlands such as saltwater swamps and tidal salt marshes protect coastal areas from storms that could destroy beaches and homes. Wetland ecosystems act as natural water-treatment facilities: the plants, fungi, and algae of a wetland filter water that drains and overflows from towns and farms, cleansing the water.

Saltwater marshland

CAN **CROPS BE GROWN IN WETLANDS?**

The most well-known wetland crop is rice, which is grown in many parts of the world, particularly India and China. It grows best in flooded fields called paddies. Another crop is Canadian wild rice, a traditional food of Native Americans.

Planting rice

Wetland forest

HOW DO **WETLANDS BECOME DAMAGED?**

When the soil is drained, or too much water is pumped out from the land nearby, wetlands suffer because the water table is lowered. They are also easily damaged by pollution: chemicals released from factories find their way into streams, upsetting the natural chemical balance.

WHAT KIND OF **PLANTS AND ANIMALS LIVE IN WETLANDS?**

In swamps and marshes, insects such as butterflies to mosquitoes, are the most common wetland animals. Some animals, such as shrimp, live in tidal marshes. Marine fish, such as striped bass, enter coastal wetlands to spawn. Oysters live in reefs, and crocodiles in saltwater marshes. Wetlands are valuable for fisheries, where fish are raised to sell.

Rapid-FIRE **?**

WHY DO WE FIND **DRAGONFLIES IN WETLANDS?**

Dragonflies lay their eggs in or near water.

Female emperor dragonfly

WHAT IS A **WATER HYACINTH?**

A fast-growing, floating weed with beautiful mauve flowers. It grows and multiplies very quickly, however, and can choke waterways.

Water hyacinth

WHERE WOULD YOU FIND A **TERRAPIN?**

In a swamp.

Diamondback terrapin

WHY ARE MOUNTAINS IMPORTANT?

Mountains capture moisture from the air and from the snow that falls on them. This moisture flows into streams and rivers that supply water to the land, helping people grow food crops. The water continues to flow and eventually reaches the ocean. Mountains are the starting point of many rivers, and an important part of the water cycle that supports life on Earth.

The Himalayas in Asia

Big? WHAT ARE MOUNTAIN ECOSYSTEMS?

Mountain ecosystems have a great variety of plant and animal species (depending upon the altitude and the nature of the mountain range). No two mountain ranges are the same: Some are icy, others face the heat of the Sun at the equator. The Himalayas in Asia are the highest mountains in the world, with a very different ecology compared to the Tibesti Mountains in Africa's central Sahara Desert. Mountain ecosystems can be quite fragile since they may be sites of volcanic eruptions and earthquakes.

WHAT IS A GRASS MOUNTAIN?

It is a steep slope covered with low vegetation and grass. The Allgäu Alps of Germany are grass mountains, popular with trekkers. Scotland is also famous for its grass mountains.

Grass mountain, Glencoe, Scotland

WHAT KINDS OF ANIMALS LIVE IN THE MOUNTAINS?

Mountains are mostly bitterly cold, windy, and lack water; it is a challenge to survive in such conditions. Yet many animals live on mountains—grazing animals such as goats, chamois, ibex, and yaks, as well as predators like pumas and snow leopards.

Snow leopard

HOW DO **FLOWERS BLOOM IN THE VERY SHORT MOUNTAIN SUMMER?**

Glacial buttercups and alpine roses spread the process of flowering over years. Since the opportunity to bloom is short, alpine flowers develop their buds in the previous summer. The buds lie dormant during the winter. Then, when the snow thaws and summer arrives, the plants bloom.

Alpine roses

Melting snows feed a mountain stream.

ARE THERE **BIRDS IN THE MOUNTAINS?**

Yes, hundreds of varieties. For example, the golden eagle and wrens of the USA's Rocky Mountains; the Andean goose and the condor of South America's Andes; the snowcock and griffon vulture of the Himalayas; and the Eurasian jay and dunnock of the Caucasian Mountains.

CAN **PLANTS SURVIVE IN COLD MOUNTAINS?**

Plants have evolved to survive the extreme cold. The Alpine edelweiss protects itself with woolly hairs, while other plants grow thick, waxy leaves. The Himalayan saussurea thistle is covered with dense wool to minimize damage from frost and the ultraviolet radiation of harsh sunlight found at a high altitude.

Edelweiss flower

Rapid-FIRE ?

WHAT IS AN IBEX?

A mountain goat.

Ibex

WHICH ANIMAL IS CALLED THE "BOAT OF THE TIBETAN PLATEAU"?

The yak.

Yak

DO **FIR TREES LOSE THEIR LEAVES IN WINTER?**

No; they are evergreens.

WHAT LIVES IN A DESERT?

Deserts can be both hot and cold. They are very dry and receive little rain. Some animals and plants have adapted to survive the extreme heat and dry conditions. Many plants are partly submerged in the ground or grow underground to beat the heat. Small mammals live in burrows and emerge only at night when it is cooler.

The Sahara Desert

WHAT ARE BURROWERS?

Desert hedgehogs, fennecs, jerboas—these are a few of the small animals who deal with the desert heat by resting in burrows or taking shelter under stones. The fennec fox has big ears to help it keep cool by radiating heat.

Fennec fox

Big? HOW DO PLANTS FIND WATER IN THE DESERT?

Desert plants

Desert plants have adapted to survive on whatever little moisture they get. Some, like cacti, have no leaves and a very thick skin to reduce water loss. Some plants have special fibers in their branches to store water. At times, during a severe drought, plants may even shed their branches to hold on to moisture. Even if the surface of the desert is dry, deep underground there is water, and plants can grow very long roots to reach it.

ARE THERE **LIZARDS IN THE DESERT?**

Yes. During the day they usually remain hidden under rocks or in the shade of desert plants. Lizards are well camouflaged, and become active at night, hunting and eating small insects and spiders. The thorny devil is a desert lizard which collects water from dew formed on its skin and channels it to its mouth. It also absorbs water from the damp sand through its skin.

Thorny devil

DO **BIRDS LIVE IN THE DESERT?**

Yes, but only a few. The sandgrouse is one such bird. It flies hundreds of miles at night to get to watering places, and rests throughout the day under bushes. It soaks up water in its chest feathers to help protect its young from the hot sun.

Sandgrouse

HOW DO **DESERT SCORPIONS SURVIVE?**

Desert scorpion

They live in loose particles of sand, are nocturnal, can burrow, and often lurk beneath rocks. The extra fat in their bodies helps them survive the extreme heat. When food is scarce, a scorpion can slow down its bodily functions to survive for days without eating.

Rapid-FIRE **?**

ARE **RATTLESNAKES VENOMOUS?**

Yes.

Rattlesnake

WHAT IS A **GILA MONSTER?**

A Mexican desert lizard.

Gila monster

WHAT IS A **DROMEDARY?**

An Arabian camel with one hump.

Dromedary

WHICH ANIMAL IS CALLED THE **"SHIP OF THE DESERT"?**

The camel.

DOES ONLY GRASS GROW IN GRASSLANDS?

From a distance, grasslands look green and fairly uniform. A closer inspection would reveal many different varieties of plants, even among grasses. As many as 80 species of plants can exist in one square yard of grassland! The shallow soil of grasslands, with porous rocks beneath, allows the little rain that falls to drain away quickly. Grassland flowers are tiny and plentiful: orchids, pansies, vetches, and worts are some examples.

Mongolian grasslands, China

Rapid-FIRE ?

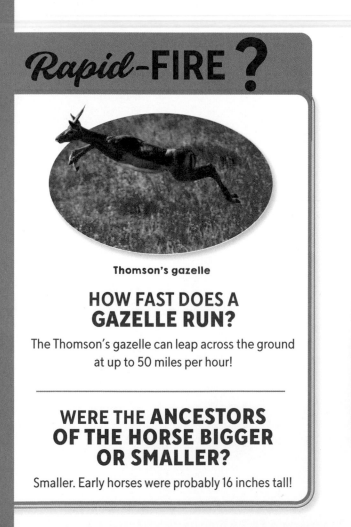

Thomson's gazelle

HOW FAST DOES A GAZELLE RUN?

The Thomson's gazelle can leap across the ground at up to 50 miles per hour!

WERE THE ANCESTORS OF THE HORSE BIGGER OR SMALLER?

Smaller. Early horses were probably 16 inches tall!

WHAT IS THE DIFFERENCE BETWEEN A BUFFALO AND A BISON?

Though both are large, hoofed mammals, they are strikingly different. A bison has an enormous head and a big shoulder hump, while buffaloes have no humps and have large, curved horns. Buffaloes belong to South Asia and Africa, while bison are found in North America and Europe.

Cape buffalo

European bison

ARE **GRAZING ANIMALS** GOOD FOR GRASSLANDS?

Yes. Different animals feed on particular plant species, so a variety of plants can flourish. Wildebeest, gazelles, zebras, and bison eat a mixture of plants, and trample the soil with their hooves, creating more spaces for plants to grow and spread. The animal droppings help nourish the plants.

Zebras in the African savannah

WHAT ARE SOME **GRASSLAND BIRDS?**

Bustards, owls, eagles, floricans, quails, warblers, and many other species are grassland specialists. They feed on insects and mammals that live within this grassy environment and build nests that are well camouflaged and hidden among the grasses.

Bustard in the Kruger National Park

Big **?** WHAT IS A **GRASSLAND ECOSYSTEM?**

Common blue wildebeest

Grasslands are home to many wild plants, and include a variety of small and tall grasses, such as tussock grass, meadow grass, and bluegrass. Steppe, pampas, veldt, and downs are types of grasslands found in different parts of the world. Grasslands do not have woody trees. Adonis flowers, anemones, delphiniums, scabious, echinaceas, sunflowers, and blazing stars are examples of flowers found in different types of grasslands. Grazing animals that feed on grass, such as antelopes, buffaloes, and horses thrive in grasslands, and so do predators like lions and cheetahs.

WHAT IS TUNDRA?

The word "tundra" means "treeless mountain tract." This treeless region is found in the Arctic and on the tops of mountains. Tundra is mostly covered in snow throughout the year. The weather is extreme: very cold and windy with little rainfall. Vast areas of tundra stretch through the north of Canada, Siberia, and Scandinavia and into Greenland.

Rapid-FIRE?

WHAT FLOWER BLOOMS NEAR THE NORTH POLE?

The Arctic poppy.

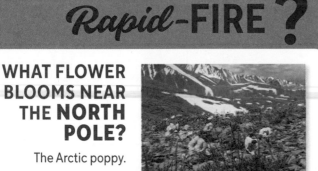

Arctic poppy

ARE ANTARCTIC LICHENS THE WORLD'S OLDEST LIVING THINGS?

Probably, since they are at least 10,000 years old!

Arctic lichen

WHY IS SNOW PINK IN ANTARCTICA?

Algae living just below the surface of the snow turn it pink.

Penguins in pink snow

WHICH BEAR PROWLS THE ARCTIC?

The polar bear is a white bear specially adapted to live in the extreme climate of the Arctic. Dense fur, a thick hide, and a layer of fat protect its body from the cold. It also has very good vision, hearing, and sense of smell, and is an excellent swimmer. It feeds on seals.

Polar bear

WHAT IS UNIQUE ABOUT THE SNOWY OWL?

The snowy owl is a large white owl living in the Arctic that is active during the day, unlike other owls. It moves around, and can be found in Arctic regions of Alaska, Canada, and Eurasia. A snowy owl swallows its prey whole. It lays up to 11 eggs at a time, but will not lay any eggs if food is in short supply.

Snowy owl

The Arctic tundra

HOW DO MOUNTAIN GOATS CLIMB?

Mountain goats are extremely nimble. They can climb the steepest slopes, and leap from crag to crag with astounding precision. The secret of their agility is in their hooves, which have sharp edges that dig into rock crevices and slightly hollow soles that act as suction pads.

Mountain goat

DOES A MOUNTAIN HARE'S COAT CHANGE IN WINTER?

Yes, it does. A mountain hare's coat is called "pelage." It turns from brown or gray to white in winter. This helps the hare hide in snow, and protects it from predators. Only the ear tip remains black. These nocturnal animals survive the winter by eating heather.

Arctic hare in its winter coat

Big? WHAT LIVES IN THE TUNDRA ECOSYSTEM?

Since the tundra ecosystem has no large trees, the only plants are dwarf trees and shrubs, such as heathers. There are also some grasses and small plants. In the Arctic it is bitterly cold for nine months of the year, but a very short summer brings over 900 species of plant to life, including wildflowers such as Arctic poppies. Grasses and sedges, mosses and lichens also thrive. Musk oxen, polar bears, Arctic foxes, gray wolves, snow geese, caribou, mountain goats, and sheep, Arctic hares, and squirrels are some of the animals that can live in this extremely cold and difficult terrain.

Caribou

Arctic fox

Gray wolves

Cold tundra landscape

WHAT IS A FRESHWATER ECOSYSTEM?

Freshwater ecosystems include rivers, streams, lakes, ponds, springs, and wetlands. Fresh water is a precious resource and its ecosystems sustain hundreds of thousands of plants, animals and microbes (microscopic forms of life). Life on Earth depends on fresh water, so the health of this ecosystem is vital.

HOW DO RIVER PLANTS SURVIVE WATER CURRENTS?

Plants have adapted to withstand the force of flowing rivers and streams. They have a very strong root system that helps them hold on firmly to their place. Plants also have leaves that are feathery and streamlined, and offer least resistance to flowing water so that they do not get pushed around. Their stems are long, supple, and slender for maximum flexibility and reach.

Water plants can grow in fast-flowing rivers.

Big ? WHAT KIND OF LIFE DO RIVERS AND LAKES SUPPORT?

Trout are freshwater fish.

Plants that live in water are called aquatic plants. Water lilies and water hyacinths have adapted to a life in water. The water lily's leaves are turned up at the edges to help the plant float like a boat. Reeds, rushes, and papyrus are grasslike water plants. Living in, or near, rivers and lakes are many kinds of small animals, such as voles, water rats, and otters; birds, including kingfishers and herons; insects such as dragonflies and water boatmen; and many kinds of fish and amphibians.

A slow-moving river supports a wealth of plant and animal life.

HOW DOES A KINGFISHER CATCH FISH?

The kingfisher waits patiently on a perch, watching the flowing water. If it sees a fish, it dives straight into the water in the blink of an eye and, with its pointed, knife-sharp beak, captures the prey and flies with incredible speed back to its perch to eat.

Common kingfisher

WHAT IS UNIQUE ABOUT HERONS?

Herons are nonswimming freshwater birds. Their long legs enable them to wade through water and prey on insects, worms, fish, and reptiles. They are excellent flyers and can hunt during both day and night.

WHY ARE OTTERS SPECIAL?

River otters are small, with soft, dense fur, webbed feet, and strong tails. The dense fur provides perfect waterproofing—no wonder otters obsessively clean and groom their fur all the time. They are very good hunters, and can crack open a shellfish using a rock.

River otter

Rapid-FIRE?

WHAT DO WATER VOLES EAT?

Waterside plants.

Water vole feeding

WHERE DO BEAVERS LIVE?

In island lodges they build using branches plastered with mud. They often dam rivers to increase the water level near their lodges.

A beaver beside its lodge

HOW DO WATER PLANTS SPREAD THEIR POLLEN?

Mostly by insects, but in some cases by floating it out on the water.

HOW DEEP IS A DEEP SEA?

Oceans have an average depth of 2.1 miles. About 70 percent of Earth is covered by oceans, and the deep sea covers 53 percent of that ocean area. The deepest point in the ocean is Challenger Deep (at one end of the Marianas Trench) at about 36,000 ft—that's deep enough to fit Mount Everest with space to spare!

CAN OCEAN FISH BE VENOMOUS?

Yes, many are. They carry venom in their glands, and can bite, sting, or stab through fins, spikes, or fangs. The reef stonefish is one of the most venomous. It shoots a venom from its spine, which can be fatal for humans.

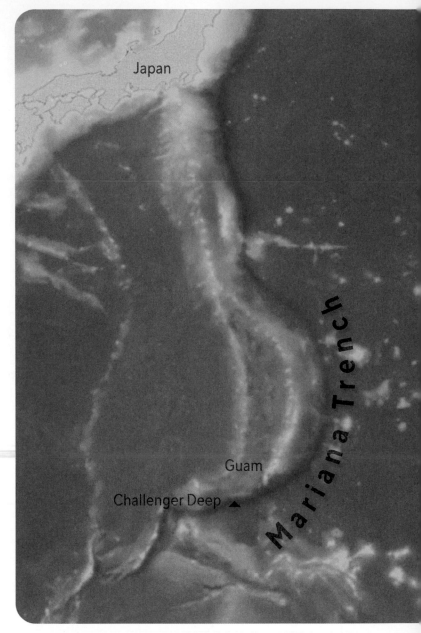

Japan

Mariana Trench

Guam

Challenger Deep ▲

The deepest part of the ocean

Big? DOES LIFE EXIST IN THE DEEP SEA?

Yes, different creatures live at different depths in the ocean. The deep sea is the largest ecosystem on Earth. It is mostly dark and cold, with enormous pressure created by the huge volume of water. Sunlight is limited, and only creatures that are specially adapted to darkness can survive.

Jellyfish

WHERE DO WHALES LIVE?

Whales are marine mammals that are completely adapted to living in the ocean. Sperm whales can easily dive 328 ft deep to hunt for squid. Blue whales, over 98 ft long and weighing over 99 tons, are the largest animals on Earth.

Sperm whales in the Caribbean

Rapid-FIRE?

WHICH WHALE IS FAMOUS FOR ITS SONG?

The humpback whale.

Humpback whale

WHICH FISH CAN BLOW ITSELF UP TO THREE TIMES ITS SIZE?

The puffer fish.

Puffer fish

CAN ANY FISH FLY OVER WATER?

Flying fish can jump out of the water and glide for a distance of 650 feet.

Flying fish

WHICH IS THE FIERCEST SHARK?

The great white shark is the most fearsome. This big fish can grow up to 20 feet long. It has strong jaws and a double row of razor-sharp teeth that can rip through a steel sheet. Great whites have about 300 sharp teeth, randomly placed in seven rows. They can swim at speeds of up to 37 miles per hour.

Great white shark

WHAT IS PHYTOPLANKTON?

It is an algae that grows on the ocean's surface. It needs sunlight to grow and contains chlorophyll, which converts sunlight to energy by photosynthesis. Phytoplankton is food for a lot of marine life, such as shrimp, snails, jellyfish, and even whales. It is believed to carry out 50 percent of Earth's photosynthesis, and so is the most important producer of oxygen.

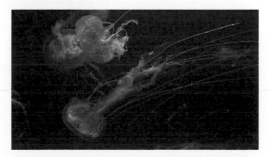

Phytoplankton and jellyfish in an aquarium

DO MARINE MAMMALS LIVE IN THE OCEAN?

Yes, and they are divided into two main groups. One is made up of animals such as seals, sea lions, and walruses, all of which live in cold places and have both fur and a thick layer of fat called blubber to keep them warm. The other group contains whales, dolphins, and porpoises, animals that don't have fur, only blubber.

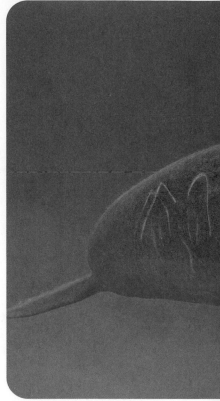

Dugong in tropical ocean water

HOW DOES A SEAL DIFFER FROM A SEA LION?

Seals and sea lions both have streamlined bodies and flippers instead of limbs. But sea lions have tiny ear flaps, while seals have only ear openings. Sea lions can fold their back flippers under the body to help them move on land. Seals cannot do this—they drag themselves along.

Sea lion

Seal

Big? WHAT IS INTERESTING ABOUT SEA LIONS, WALRUSES, AND SEALS?

Seals, sea lions, and walruses are agile swimmers, but unlike whales and dolphins, they can come up on land—although they don't really walk but move with a kind of waddle. In spring and summer, thousands of seals crowd together on the shore to breed in enormous colonies. Interestingly, although they are two different creatures, seals and sea lions look similar and both mostly feed on fish, but also eat shellfish. Walruses are huge and look a little like overgrown seals. They have huge tusks and face whiskers.

Walrus

Rapid-FIRE ?

WHY IS A **SEA LION CALLED A "LION"?**

Some species, such as the South American and the Steller, actually have a lionlike mane.

South American sea lion

WHICH SEAL IS THE MOST **FEROCIOUS HUNTER?**

The Antarctic leopard seal.

Antarctic leopard seal

HOW DOES A **WALRUS SURVIVE A COLD ARCTIC WINTER?**

Layers of blubber keep it warm in temperatures as low as -350 °F.

HOW BIG IS A WALRUS?

A large male walrus can be more than 10 feet long—twice the length of a bathtub—and weigh up to 3,700 lbs—as much as a large car. Females are smaller, averaging 8.8 ft in length and weighing about 1,800 lbs. Both males and females have tusks that are used for mating displays and to fight off attackers.

Male walrus

DO **SEA COWS LOOK LIKE COWS?**

Two types of plant-eating seals—dugongs and manatees—are known as sea cows. They don't look like cows, but they do move just as slowly. Dugongs are found in the warm coastal waters around Africa and Asia; manatees are found in warm coastal rivers in southeastern USA, the West Indies, and northern South America.

Manatee in Florida, USA

WHAT ARE ROOKERIES?

Seals spend most of their lives in the ocean, but come ashore to give birth and nurse their babies. They stay on land for several weeks in large colonies called rookeries.

Fur seal rookery

WHAT ARE TURTLES?

The name "turtle" is used for about 200 different species, all of which are reptiles with shells that are fused with their ribs and vertebrae. The species that live on land, however, are known as tortoises. Turtles spend most of their lives in water, only coming to land to lay eggs. There are seven species of marine turtles, which all have flipperlike front legs and webbed hind feet.

Big? WHAT IS THE DIFFERENCE BETWEEN FRESHWATER AND MARINE TURTLES?

Red-eared terrapin

Most marine turtles are bigger than their freshwater cousins, which are also known as terrapins. Unlike terrapins, marine turtles cannot retract their necks and heads inside their shell. They are adapted to spending most of their life at sea because their legs cannot really support their weight—females crawl up the beach only to lay their eggs. Terrapins are found in rivers, ponds, and lakes. While they do have webbed feet, they can walk and do spend time on land.

HOW DO TURTLE HATCHLINGS SURVIVE?

Female turtles lay their eggs in holes they dig on sandy beaches before returning to the ocean. The eggs hatch in about 60 days, usually at  night to give the tiny babies the best chance to avoid predators as they scurry down the beach and into the water.

Hatchlings running down to the ocean

HOW DOES THE HINGED TERRAPIN PROTECT ITSELF?

This native of South Africa not only closes its hinged shell after pulling its head inside, it also releases a foul smell from its musk glands to keep predators away.

Hinged terrapin

Sea turtle above a coral reef

WHERE IS THE **HAWKSBILL TURTLE FOUND?**

The hawksbill gets its name because its mouth resembles the sharp beak of a hawk. The turtle, which has a beautifully colored and patterned shell, lives among the coral reefs of the Pacific, Indian and Atlantic Oceans. It can grow to about 3.7 feet, more than half the length of a full-size bed, and weigh almost 155 pounds.

The hawksbill

HOW BIG IS THE **LEATHERBACK?**

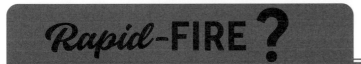

The largest of all the turtles is the leatherback, which can grow up to 5.2 ft long and weigh about 795 pounds—almost as much as a horse. Unlike other turtles, its shell is not hard but slightly flexible with an almost rubberlike feel. It can stay underwater for over an hour and dive to a depth of about 4,200 ft.

The leatherback

Rapid-FIRE **?**

Sea turtle breathing

DO AQUATIC **TURTLES BREATHE UNDERWATER?**

No, they don't. They must come to the surface to breathe air.

Baby turtles

HOW DO **HATCHLINGS FIND THEIR WAY TO THE OCEAN?**

The natural light across the ocean horizon guides them out.

Hawksbill feeding

WHICH **TURTLE FEEDS ON SEA SPONGES?**

The hawksbill.

IS A **TURTLE'S SHELL A BONE?**

It is made of around 60 bones covered with keratin, the same material that makes up your fingernails.

DO WHALES AND DOLPHINS SWIM LIKE FISH?

Mammals that spend all their lives in water, such as whales, dolphins, and porpoises, are known as cetaceans. While they look like fish, their swimming styles differ because they don't really have fins, but very well-adapted limbs. So, cetaceans move their bodies up and down, while fish use horizontal movements to propel themselves in water.

A humpback whale jumps out of the water.

DO WHALES BREATHE UNDERWATER?

Whales can stay underwater for long periods but must eventually come up to the surface to breathe through a blowhole on top of their heads. Normally whales can hold their breath for about an hour, though the longest known dive was by a Cuvier's beaked whale, lasting all of 2 hours and 17 minutes!

A whale surfacing to breathe

HOW DOES A BLUE WHALE EAT?

Hanging from the blue whale's upper jaw are plates of a bristly material called baleen. When the whale opens its mouth, water flows in, carrying lots of krill with it. When the whale shuts its mouth, the water filters out through the baleen, leaving the krill trapped for the whale to swallow.

Big?
HOW DO WHALES AND DOLPHINS KEEP IN TOUCH?

Bottlenose dolphin

They use a low-frequency booming sound to communicate—fin whales can hear each other from 530 miles away! The humpback whale sings—a series of high whistles and low rumbles that may last from five minutes to as long as 35 minutes. All cetaceans are social, and dolphins live in schools of up to 300 strong, keeping in touch by making a range of sounds, most of which are too high for the human ear to hear.

WHICH IS THE **LARGEST DOLPHIN?**

The orca, commonly known as a killer whale.

Orca

DO **DOLPHINS TALK?**

They are very talkative and constantly click, bark, and chatter to communicate.

A pod of dolphins

WHICH **WHALE HAS TEETH?**

The sperm whale.

Sperm whale

DO **CETACEANS HAVE HAIR?**

Yes, but it is usually restricted to just a few strands on their heads and under their chins.

ARE **DOLPHINS SOCIAL ANIMALS?**

Dolphins are very friendly, playful and intelligent animals. They form strong social relationships, with close mother-child bonds. Mating pairs seem to stay together for life. Leaps, somersaults, and spins help knit groups of dolphins together.

Dolphins at play

WHY DO SOME **WHALES MIGRATE?**

Whales, such as the humpbacks, migrate—that is, travel seasonally—to find the best conditions for feeding and breeding. They spend much of the year feeding in the waters of the Arctic and Antarctic, where there is plenty of krill to eat, but travel to warmer waters near the equator when it is time to give birth.

Humpback whale mother and calf

ARE FISH VERTEBRATES?

Yes, fish have a spinal cord surrounded by bone or cartilage—the characteristic of vertebrate animals. Fish can live in fresh or salt water. Most fish are cold-blooded and have gills that extract oxygen from the water around them. Fish don't have limbs; they have fins and have evolved a scaly, streamlined body for swimming. Almost half of all species of vertebrate animals in the world are fish.

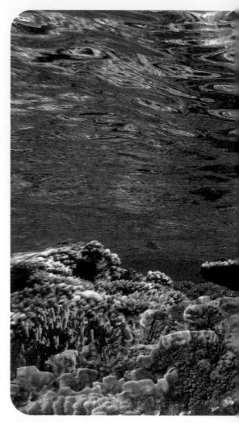
Emperor angelfish amid coral

WHICH IS THE FIERCEST FRESHWATER FISH?

The piranha, which is found in the rivers of tropical South America. There are about 60 kinds of piranha, all of which have strong jaws with sharp, triangular teeth. Piranhas are about one and a half times the size of a bowling pin, and while they are mostly scavengers, a school can kill and eat a large mammal very quickly.

A school of piranhas

HOW DO FRESHWATER AND SALTWATER FISH DIFFER?

Big?

Freshwater trout

The basic difference is in the habitat, especially the amount of salt in the water. Freshwater fish are found in rivers, lakes, and ponds. Saltwater fish live in marine environments, such as coral reefs and the deep ocean. Freshwater fish retain salts in their bodies to make up for the low salt levels in the water around them, while sea fish can filter and get rid of the excess salt they take in. Pike, trout, guppy, and angelfish are some of the fish found in fresh water. Examples of saltwater fish include clown fish, seahorses, eels, sharks, and tuna.

CAN FISH **SURVIVE AMONG POISONOUS ANEMONES?**

Small fish with bright orange, white-barred bodies called anemone fish, or clown fish, live in tropical waters among colonies of sea anemones, whose tentacles carry a powerful sting fatal to other fish. The anemone fish have a mucous covering that makes them immune to the poison and so they find a safe home among the anemones.

Anemone fish

ARE **PUFFER FISH POISONOUS?**

Yes, they are. Many species of puffer fish are among the most poisonous of all fish. Concentrated around their internal organs is a substance called tetrodotoxin, and a single puffer fish has enough of this toxin to kill 30 adult humans! Despite this, cleaned and carefully prepared puffer fish is a delicacy in Japan.

Puffer fish

WHY DO **FLYING FISH "FLY"?**

Flying fish don't really fly; they glide on extra-large fins, which act as "wings." They usually do this to escape danger. Once the flying fish has built up speed under the water, the fish lifts its fins and is able to glide above the surface for a short distance.

Flying Cypselurus fish

Rapid-FIRE ?

WHICH FISH **CAN LEAP UP A WATERFALL?**

Salmon.

Salmon at a waterfall

WHY **DON'T FISH SINK?**

They have an air bag inside their body called a swim bladder that helps them float.

Swim bladder

A fish's internal air bag

HOW **FAST CAN A SAILFISH SWIM?**

At more than 65 miles per hour.

Sailfish

Stingrays in shallow water

WHAT DO SHARKS AND RAYS HAVE IN COMMON?

Sharks and rays belong to a group of fish that have larger brains than other fish, and whose skeletons are made of cartilage rather than bone. Cartilage is softer and more flexible. Also, sharks and rays do not all reproduce in the same way as other fish. Some species give birth to babies, while some keep the eggs in their uterus until the young are born. Others leave their eggs attached to rocks, seaweed, or coral reefs, where they will eventually hatch.

Big? DO SHARKS AND RAYS LOOK ALIKE?

They look different. Unlike the sharks' long, slender, typical fish-shaped bodies, rays have a flat, disklike shape and their gills and mouth are located on the underside of their bodies. They have enlarged fins that extend out like wings and when they swim, they look as if they are "flying" through the water. While sharks take in water for oxygen through their open mouths as they swim, rays have openings called spiracles on the upper head to take in water and pass it to the gill chambers. Also, unlike sharks, which have tail fins, rays have long, slender tails.

Gray reef sharks

DO ALL **SHARKS** HUNT LARGE PREY?

No, the whale shark and the basking shark, which are the largest and second-largest fish in the world, eat only tiny, shrimplike marine animals. They have developed a special sievelike structure in their mouths to filter these from the water.

Whale shark

DOES A **STINGRAY STING?**

Stingrays get their name from the sharp spine or barb near the base of their tails. If stepped on, the spine—which is sometimes venomous—can cause a nasty wound.

Southern stingray

HOW MANY **GROUPS OF** RAYS ARE THERE?

There are four broad groups of rays: electric rays have electric organs that store power and can deliver a powerful shock; stingrays have long, whiplike tails with stingy spines; sawfish have snouts that have evolved into a blade; while skates are the only rays that lay eggs.

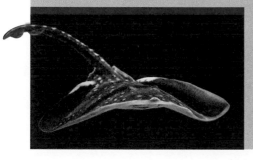

Flat skate fish

HOW BIG IS THE **GREAT** WHITE SHARK?

Male great whites grow to about 13 feet long, while females can measure up to 20 feet—the height of a giraffe! Found in warm oceans all over the world, they are fierce hunters with large, jagged-edged teeth. They feed mostly on large fish and marine mammals such as sea lions, porpoises, and even whales.

Great white shark

Rapid-FIRE ?

WHAT DO **TIGER SHARKS** HUNT?

Fish, seals, birds, turtles, and other, smaller sharks.

Tiger shark

HOW WIDE IS THE **BLUE-SPOTTED STINGRAY?**

Nearly 27 inches wide.

Blue-spotted stingray

WHICH SHARK HAS A **MALLET-SHAPED HEAD?**

The hammerhead shark.

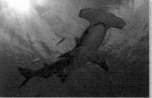

Hammerhead shark

DO **RAYS LIVE NEAR THE** WATER SURFACE?

No, they are bottom dwellers.

WHY ARE ANIMALS KNOWN AS FAUNA?

"Fauna" is a word for all the animal life within a region or period of time. The word comes from Greek mythology and roughly means "creatures of the wild." The naturalist Carl Linnaeus was the first to use this term in 1974 in the title of his book *Fauna Svecica,* which means the "wildlife of Sweden."

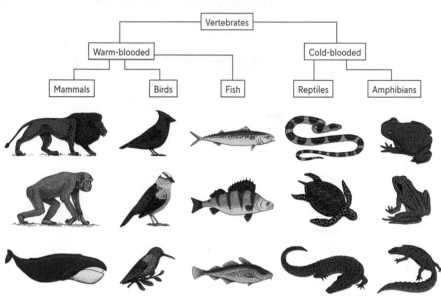

How vertebrates are classified

WHAT IS IN THE ANIMAL KINGDOM?

The animal kingdoem refers to all animals that live on land, water, high up on trees, or can even fly. They can be so small that they are hardly visible to the naked eye, and can also be huge. Most of them are very mobile and active. They get their energy from food, which can be plants or other animals. Animals are not grouped according to their sizes, but on the basis of other factors: their bone structure, how they reproduce and take care of their babies, how they move, how they breathe, and also whether they stay on land or in water (or sometims both).

The animal kingdom

WHAT ARE **PREDATORS AND PREY?**

When one animal kills another for food, it is called predation. The animal which kills is called a predator, and the animal which gets killed is known as prey. Predators often have special skills for hunting, with highly tuned vision, hearing, and sense of smell. Many have sharp claws and jaws to grab hold of and tear the body of the prey. Predators can act in a group or kill alone. At times they hide and wait to catch their prey off guard in an ambush killing.

Predator and prey

WHAT IS **HARMFUL TO THE ANIMAL KINGDOM?**

Destruction of natural habitats

Although natural disasters and sudden changes on Earth's surface, such as earthquakes, volcanoes, and wildfires, can hurt the animal kingdom, human-led changes, such as the cutting down of forests, deliberate forest fires, water and air pollution, have also severely affected wild animal habitats across the world.

WHAT IS **LIVESTOCK?**

Animals kept by humans to help them in farm work, carrying loads, traveling from one place to another, and producing goods for everyday needs, like milk, fur, wool, and leather are livestock animals. Cattle, sheep, pigs, goats, horses, donkeys, mules, buffaloes, camels, and llamas are livestock. Farmed birds like chicken, turkeys, and geese are poultry, not livestock.

Sheep   **Pigs**

Camel

Goat

Rapid-FIRE **?**

WHAT ANIMAL LIVES THE **LONGEST?**

Sponges live for a very long time, often thousands of years!

Sponges

WHICH **ANIMAL HAS THE SHORTEST LIFE SPAN?**

An adult female mayfly lives for less than five minutes!

Adult mayfly

WHICH ANIMAL HAS **EXISTED SINCE THE TIME OF DINOSAURS?**

Cockroaches. They are at least 200 million years old and may have even been alive before dinosaurs.

HOW LONG HAVE **ANIMALS EXISTED ON EARTH?**

For 1.2 billion years.

WHAT ARE INSECTS?

Insects are small animals with no bones. An insect's body is protected by a hard outer covering called an exoskeleton. The body has three segments: head, thorax, and abdomen. The head has eyes—which can have six to 30,000 lenses—and a pair of antennae to feel, taste, and smell things. The thorax has wings and legs. The abdomen includes systems for digesting food.

A jewel bug

WHAT ARE DRAGONFLIES?

Dragonflies are large, fast-flying insects that can dart at speeds up to 37 miles per hour. Their four wings move independently of one another, and make a rattling sound. Dragonflies can also fly backward.

A dragonfly

Rapid-FIRE?

WHICH IS THE SMALLEST INSECT?

A fairy fly is just 0.2 mm long!

WHICH IS THE LONGEST INSECT?

The stick insect from Borneo is over 10 inches long.

HOW STRONG ARE ANTS?

An ant can lift 50 times its own weight—that is like a human lifting a truck!

Soil turned by ants

HOW DO ANTS HELP US?

Ants dig and build underground nests. This allows air into the soil, which improves air, water, and nutrient circulation for plants.

Red fire ant

ARE RED FIRE ANTS IMPORTANT?

Yes, very. They feed on fleas, ticks, termites, cockroaches, and mosquito larva.

WHAT ARE TERMITES?

Termites are insects that live in very big colonies in the tropical areas of the world. They feed on dead plants and wood. The huge mounds of dust and saliva they build to live in even have air conditioning. Some termite mounds can be 30 feet tall—the height of five people!

Termites

Honeybee

WHAT ARE BUTTERFLIES AND MOTHS?

Butterflies and moths are both part of a big group of insects that have wings covered in tiny dustlike scales. Butterflies are usually brightly colored, and fly during the day. They have a thin, hairless body and a pair of antennae each with a small bulb at the end. Moths tend to be duller in color so they are camouflaged when they rest on trees and leaves during the day. They have antennae and plump, hairy bodies.

Common tiger butterfly

Big **?** WHAT ARE BEES AND WHY ARE THEY IMPORTANT?

Bees are flying insects found on every continent on the Earth (except Antarctica), and in every habitat where there are insect-pollinated flowering plants. There are over 16,000 species of bees! Bees like honeybees and bumblebees live in colonies, in hives, or nests. Many fruits and vegetables that humans eat are pollinated by bees. Even food eaten by cattle and other farm animals needs bees for pollination. So, when we are eating plants directly or meat from an animal that has had a diet of plants, we depend on bees for our food.

WHAT ARE REPTILES?

Reptiles are scaly-skinned animals such as crocodiles, lizards, and snakes. They are cold-blooded, which means they depend on the Sun for warmth and have to move back and forth between warm and cold places to maintain the right temperature in their bodies. They may spend hours basking in the sun to gain enough energy to hunt for food. Reptiles can survive on limited food, but they cannot live in cold places.

A chameleon

Rapid-FIRE?

HOW VENOMOUS IS A KING COBRA'S BITE?

A single bite has enough poison to kill 20 people or an adult elephant!

King cobra

CAN LIZARDS CHANGE COLOR?

Chameleons change color, both to camouflage and to communicate.

Chameleon

HOW DIFFERENT ARE PYTHONS AND BOAS?

Pythons have one more bone in the head, and some more teeth, but the big difference is that the python lays eggs, while boas give birth to live young snakes.

WHAT IS AN ANACONDA?

Anacondas are boa constrictors found in swamps and marshes of Amazon rainforests.

WHAT IS SPECIAL ABOUT GABOON VIPERS?

These snakes have fangs up to two inches long—the longest among snakes. The fangs are in the front of the mouth, and hinge back into the mouth when not in use. Their venom is very strong, and they are known to eat big rats, and even antelopes.

Gaboon viper

WHAT IS A FRILLED-NECKED LIZARD?

This Australian lizard has an enormous frill. Normally the frill hangs limp, but when the lizard is threatened, it spreads out up to nine inches, and makes the lizard look three times as large and twice as dangerous.

Frilled-necked lizard

HOW MANY KINDS OF **LIZARDS** ARE THERE?

There are probably over 3,000 species of lizards. These belong to different groups, such as geckos, iguanas, skinks, and chameleons. Most lizards have four limbs and a tail. Many lizards can shed their tails to escape a predator. The Komodo dragon, which lives on some Southeast Asian islands, is the world's largest lizard. Up to 10 feet long, it can hunt down wild pigs and small deer.

Komodo dragon

WHAT IS A **TAIPAN?**

The taipan is a poisonous snake from Australia. It can grow up to 10 feet long, which is huge for a venomous snake. It belongs to the same family as the cobra, and has venom in its front fangs.

Taipan

Big? WHAT ARE SNAKES?

Snakes are long, limbless reptiles, living mostly in the warm regions of Earth. They are predators. They kill their prey with poison (known as venom) or by constricting (squeezing) it to death. There are about 2,500 species of snakes. Snakes have no ears and sense their prey from vibrations on the ground. They use their flickering tongue to smell. Their eyesight is poor, so they can only see things when they are close. About one-third of all snakes are venomous, but few have poison strong enough to harm humans.

Blue viper

DO AMPHIBIANS LIVE ON LAND OR IN WATER?

Amphibians live part of their lives in water and part on land. They are animals such as frogs, toads, newts, and salamanders. They begin life in water when they hatch from big clusters of jellylike eggs called spawn. At this stage they have gills to help them extract oxygen from water. As they grow, they develop lungs for breathing air, but they rarely stray very far from water, since their soft skin needs to be kept moist.

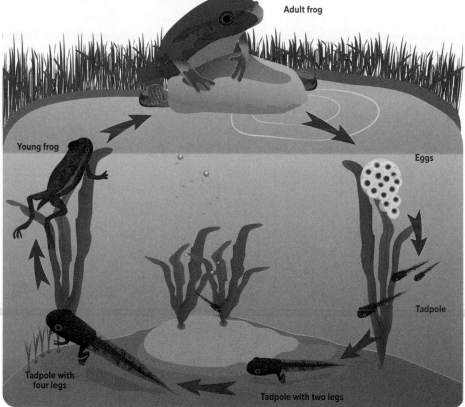

Adult frog

Young frog

Eggs

Tadpole

Tadpole with four legs

Tadpole with two legs

Life cycle of a frog

Rapid-FIRE?

Frog's eggs

WHY DO AMPHIBIANS LAY THEIR EGGS IN WATER?

So that they don't dry out.

Darwin's frog

WHICH FROG CARRIES TADPOLES IN ITS VOCAL POUCH?

The male Darwin's frog.

The Cuban tree frog

WHICH IS THE SMALLEST FROG?

The Cuban tree frog.

DO FLYING FROGS FLY?

No, they glide.

ARE NEWTS COLORFUL?

Many male newts develop bright colors and special markings during the mating season to attract females. The crested newt has a bright orange or yellow belly as well as a bumpy crest down the length of its back.

Crested newt

HOW DID THE FIRE SALAMANDER GET ITS NAME?

Fire salamanders commonly shelter underneath logs. In earlier times, when log fires were common, salamanders would run out from the logs when the fire was lit. This meant that people linked them with fire; some even believed that they were born in fires.

Fire salamander

HOW DO TREE FROGS CLIMB TREES?

On each of their long toes, tree frogs have a round, sticky pad, which allows them to cling to the undersides of leaves and to run up even the smoothest surfaces. They spend most of their lives in trees and may only come down to the ground to lay their eggs in or near water.

Red-eyed tree frog

Big?

WHAT IS THE DIFFERENCE BETWEEN FROGS AND TOADS?

Common toad

Both frogs and toads are amphibians. Frogs, however, have smooth, moist (slimy) skin and must stay fairly close to water. Most toads have rough, dry skin and they do not need to be near water. Toads are broader, heavier, and squatter to look at. Frogs have much longer and stronger hind legs and can leap much higher. Toads take smaller hops and may even crawl fast instead. Also, frogs are eaten by a number of other animals, but toad skin tastes bitter and gives out a pungent smell that discourages predators.

WHICH AMPHIBIANS LOOK LIKE LIZARDS?

Newts and salamanders. But they are not reptiles like lizards, but instead begin life in water. Newts live in temperate climates and hibernate during the winter under logs and stones. Salamanders live in warmer areas and do not need to hibernate.

WHAT IS THE DIFFERENCE BETWEEN A CROCODILE AND AN ALLIGATOR?

Alligators are rounder and fatter, with short, blunt snouts; crocodiles are more streamlined and their snouts are longer and narrower. An easy way to figure out which is which is that the fourth tooth on a crocodile's lower row of teeth can be seen even when the jaw is shut, while in alligators, the tooth disappears into pits in the upper jaw when its mouth is closed.

Nile crocodile

Sarcosuchus fossil

Big? ARE CROCODILES RELATED TO DINOSAURS?

Crocodiles may be one of the closest living links to dinosaurs. The scaly skin, teeth, claws, and the way they look are all still very much the same. The fact that they were such efficient hunters, well adapted to their environment, meant that they did not need to change very much. Their streamlined bodies, long, powerful tails and webbed feet make them very fast in the water. The Nile crocodile can grow to 20 feet in length, but the Indopacific crocodile, which lives in parts of Southeast Asia, can grow even larger.

HOW DO CROCODILES HUNT?

They usually lie and wait in shallow water until animals come to drink. Then they make a sudden lunge, grab the victim with their massive, snapping jaws, drag it into the water, and drown it.

DO CROCODILES LAY EGGS?

Yes, and they take care of them very carefully. Female crocodiles scoop out a pit in the ground then lay 30 or more eggs there, covering them up with earth or sand. The female will stay nearby, guarding the nest for about three months while the eggs are ready to hatch.

Crocodile hatchlings

American alligator

WHAT DO **CROCODILES AND ALLIGATORS EAT?**

Baby crocs and alligators will catch insects and spiders to eat. As they grow, fish and birds form a larger part of their diet. When fully grown, they will prey on anything that comes their way: fish and birds, as well as small and large mammals.

A Nile crocodile catches a wildebeest

HOW MANY SPECIES OF **CROCODILES AND ALLIGATORS ARE THERE?**

There are about 14 species of crocodiles spread throughout the tropical regions of every continent. Of the two species of alligators, the American is better known than the lower Yangtze River alligator from China.

The lower Yangtze River alligator

Rapid-FIRE ?

WHERE DO **CROCODILES LIVE?**

In rivers and swamps of the tropics.

Alligator in swampy water

HOW LONG AGO DID THE CROCODILES' ANCESTORS ROAM THE EARTH?

200 million years ago.

A *Sarcosuchus* approaches a *Huayangosaurus* (computer illustration)

DO **ALLIGATORS ESTABLISH TERRITORIES?**

Yes, and an adult alligator will frequently fight to defend it.

CAN **CROCODILES AND ALLIGATORS CLIMB TREES?**

Yes. Smaller juveniles can get as high as 25 to 30 feet.

HOW CAN YOU TELL A CAIMAN FROM A CROCODILE AND AN ALLIGATOR?

Caimans are freshwater carnivores native to Central and South America. Like other animals from the Crocodylidae family, caimans live along the edges of rivers, swamps, and other bodies of water. They are smaller than crocodiles and alligators. Caimans have U-shaped snouts, and their bottom teeth are covered when their jaws are closed, so they look more like alligators than crocodiles.

Black caiman

Big? WHAT SIZE ARE THE BIGGEST AND SMALLEST CAIMANS?

The black caiman, which can grow up to 13 feet in length, is the largest. It inhabits a very large area of the Amazon River basin from Peru to Ecuador and Guyana, and Suriname toward the east. It mostly eats fish, reptiles, and rodents, and is a ferocious, extremely dangerous predator. At about six feet in length, the smooth-fronted caiman is the smallest of the caimans. It is found in the Amazon and Orinoco River basins of South America.

Smooth-fronted caiman

WHAT IS A **GHARIAL**?

Gharials are also reptiles in the Crocodylidae family. They live in fresh water, and are only found in parts of India and Nepal. A long, sleek snout that displays rows of very sharp, flesh-tearing teeth, and a bulbous lump on the male's snout make them different from their cousins. Gharials can grow up to 20 feet in length.

Gharial

HOW DID THE **SPECTACLED CAIMAN GET ITS NAME?**

The ridge between its eyes makes it look like it is wearing eyeglasses. This reptile is found across southern Mexico and down to Brazil. It frequents quiet, mud-bottomed waters and can grow up to 8.8 feet in length.

Spectacled caiman

Rapid-FIRE **?**

HOW DO **GHARIALS REGULATE THEIR BODY TEMPERATURE?**

By basking in the sun and cooling down in water.

Gharial basking in the sun

WHAT IS SPECIAL ABOUT THE **CUVIER'S DWARF CAIMAN'S SKIN?**

It is much stronger and more inflexible than that of other caimans.

Cuvier's dwarf caiman

HOW MUCH CAN A **GHARIAL WEIGH?**

Adults weigh between 330 and 550 pounds—as much as the weight of two huge people.

HOW DO **MALE GHARIALS ATTRACT FEMALES?**

The male gharial sings and blow bubbles through the bulbous growth on its snout to attract females. This growth, which looks like a mud pot, or *ghara* (in India's Hindi language), is what gives the animal its name.

HOW DO **GHARIALS HUNT?**

Gharials are mostly fish eaters, though younger animals also eat insects and frogs. When they move their heads in the water, sensory cells in the gharials' snouts detect vibrations in the water. Their jaws, which are lined with over 100 teeth, are designed to efficiently catch fish.

The gharial's long snout

WHAT ARE MARSUPIALS?

Marsupials are mammals that give birth to live young. However, their babies are tiny and not fully formed when they are born. They develop outside their mothers' bodies, firmly attached to the nipples. Many marsupials have a flap of skin that forms a pouch where their baby will sit. There are about 300 species of marsupials, of which nearly 200 are found in Australia and surrounding islands.

A koala is not a bear at all.

Big? WHICH IS THE BEST KNOWN MARSUPIAL?

Forester kangaroo and joey

The kangaroo. Adult kangaroos eat grass and the leaves of low-growing plants, just like deer do. A kangaroo bounds along on its strong back legs at up to 30 miles per hour and can cover the length of a semitruck in one giant bound. Even when fully developed kangaroo babies, called joeys, return to the safety of the mother's pouch if startled.

DO MARSUPIALS EAT MEAT?

Yes, some do. The Tasmanian devil is the largest of the carnivorous, or meat-eating, marsupials. It is around three feet long, including the tail, and has sharp teeth and strong jaws. The devil feeds mostly on carrion—the flesh of animals that are already dead—but it does also kill prey such as birds.

Tasmanian devil

IS THE **KOALA BEAR A BEAR?**

No, it's a marsupial and not related to bears at all. Koalas live in Australia in eucalyptus forests. They feed almost entirely on eucalyptus leaves, and prefer those of only a few species. A baby koala spends its first six to seven months in the pouch and after that rides on its mother's back.

Rapid-FIRE ?

HOW MUCH DOES A **KOALA EAT?**

Around a pound of eucalyptus leaves every day.

Koala

WHAT ARE **BANDICOOTS?**

A group of small marsupials that live in Australia and New Guinea.

Australian long-nosed bandicoot

WHICH IS THE **SMALLEST MARSUPIAL?**

The mouselike ningaui, found in Australia.

Southern ningaui

WHY DOES A **WOMBAT'S POUCH HAVE A REAR ENTRANCE?**

Wombat and baby

A wombat is a small bearlike marsupial with a heavy body and short, strong legs. It uses its strong teeth and claws to dig the burrow it shelters in. The wombat's pouch opens to the rear so that it does not fill up with soil when the animal is burrowing.

DO ALL **MARSUPIALS HAVE A POUCH?**

Most female marsupials have a pouch, but not all. Some very small marsupials, such as the shrew opossums of South America, do not have a pouch. Others, such as American opossums, have simple flaps of skin around the nipples that the tiny baby can cling on to.

North American opossum

WHAT MAKES BIRDS SPECIAL?

Birds are a group of warm-blooded animals with feathers and wings that enable them to fly. They inhabit all of the world's ecosystems. Birds have highly specialized muscles and bones to steer and control their movement during flight, and they build nests to lay eggs. Birds are probably the most vibrant and colorful group of animals on the planet.

Andean condor in flight

DO **ALL BIRDS FLY?**

No, there are some birds that have lost their ability to fly through evolution. Penguins, ostriches, kiwis, kakapo, steamer ducks, weka, takahes, and cassowaries are all flightless birds, and have more feathers than birds that fly.

Cassowary

Big **?** ARE BIRDS PREDATORS?

Many birds are hunters. The smaller ones feed on worms and insects. Larger birds of prey such as hawks, eagles, owls, vultures, and falcons are called raptors and are powerful birds that catch and feed on small birds, fish, and mammals such as rabbits and even baby goats. Most are more active during the day, though owls usually hunt at night and have excellent hearing and night vision.

Long-eared owl

WHICH ARE THE LARGEST AND SMALLEST BIRDS OF PREY?

The Andean condor is the biggest. Measuring up to 43 inches in length and weighing up to 26 pounds, it has a huge wingspan at over 9 ft across. The black-thighed falconet and the Bornean falconet of Southeast Asia, with a length of 5–6 inches, are the smallest birds of prey. They feed on smaller birds and insects.

Black-thighed falconet

WHY ARE VULTURES IMPORTANT?

Vultures are scavengers, which means that they feed on animals that are already dead, acting as natural cleaners in the wild by reducing the spread of bacteria and other disease-causing microbes.

Griffon vulture

Rapid-FIRE ?

WHAT IS A GANNET?

Gannets are the largest seabirds in the North Atlantic Ocean.

Gannet

IS A PUFFIN A KIND OF PENGUIN?

No, puffins belong to a family of birds called auks, and they can fly.

Puffin

HOW FAST CAN PENGUINS SWIM?

About 8 miles per hour.

Penguin swimming underwater

WHICH ARE THE LARGEST AND THE SMALLEST BIRDS?

The largest living bird is the ostrich of Africa. An adult male ostrich can be 9 ft long and can weigh 265 pounds. The smallest bird is the bee hummingbird of Cuba. The adult female is 2.4 inches long and weighs only 2.6 g—the weight of 13 matchsticks!

Male ostrich　　　**Bee hummingbird**

ARE BIRDS VOCAL?

Almost all birds make some kind of sound. With their squawks, songs, and calls, birds can be very noisy. While baby birds chirp, adult birds create more elaborate notes. Their sounds differ from one situation with another, depending on whether they are communicating with each other or sounding an alert. Some birds make more complex, musical sounds, and are known as songbirds. There are 5,000 species of songbirds in the world. Their vocal muscles enable them to sing complex and distinct territorial songs.

The spangled cotinga whistles by vibrating special wing feathers.

Big? CAN BIRDS TALK LIKE HUMANS?

Macaw

Birds that can mimic human speech are known as talking birds. They include both captive and wild birds. Typically, some songbirds and parrots are talking birds. Parrots are very smart, and can be trained to speak many words and even full sentences. Macaws can pick up words and sounds (such as a car alarm) quickly, after hearing a sound just once, and they have a superb memory, retaining much of what they learn.

WHY DO SONGBIRDS SING?

While a caged bird may sing for no particular reason, males in the wild sing to attract females and also to announce their claim to a certain territory. Females sing in defense of territory. Chicks learn songs from parents, so a bird born in captivity may not know the detailed variation of notes a wild bird would.

CAN BIRDS MAKE SOUNDS WITH THEIR FEATHERS?

Hummingbirds are unique since they produce noises through both vocal and nonvocal means. Hummingbirds chirp and chatter, as well as creating sounds by vibrating the primary feathers in their wings. A few species of hummingbirds, like the Cuban bee, rufous, and woodstar can create a loud, high-pitched chirp with their tails!

The Cuban bee hummingbird vocalizes with its tail.

WHAT ARE BUDGERIGARS?

A long-tailed, seed-eating parrot species, budgerigars make popular pets. They are social birds, often referred to as "budgies," and can be taught to speak, whistle, and play.

Budgerigars

HOW MUCH "HUMAN TALK" CAN A BIRD LEARN?

African gray parrots, an endangered species, are highly intelligent and can be taught over 100 words, number sequences, and more. They can even recognize a human voice and relate it to a particular human face!

African gray parrot

Rapid-FIRE?

WHO IS THE LOUDEST?

The male white bellbird of the Amazon rainforest. If it released its mating call next to you, it would feel like you were standing beside a speaker at a rock concert!

White bellbird

IS THERE MORE TO A RAVEN'S CAW?

Yes, experts can detect 33 kinds of sounds in a raven's caw.

Raven cawing

WHAT IS THE DIFFERENCE BETWEEN A BIRDCALL AND BIRDSONG?

Calls are usually short, single notes, while songs have more notes and a pattern.

WHAT ARE MAMMALS?

Mammals are vertebrates—animals that have a backbone. This means that all mammals have a bony skeleton inside their bodies, which gives them a strong frame. They usually have two pairs of limbs, and organs such as a heart, lungs, a stomach, and intestines. They come in all shapes and sizes and live in a huge variety of places, from the frozen Arctic wastes to the hottest deserts on Earth.

Weasel

Big?

HOW ARE MAMMALS DIFFERENT FROM OTHER ANIMALS?

Lioness and cub

All mammals have fur on their bodies—hair is a form of fur—and they are warm-blooded. This means that they are able to keep their body temperature stable even if there are changes in their environment. Most begin life inside the mother's body and are born as well-formed babies. Mammal babies feed on their mothers' milk until they are old enough to eat solid foods.

WHAT MAKES THE ETRUSCAN SHREW INTERESTING?

Weighing less than three grams, the Etruscan shrew is the smallest known mammal on earth. A very high metabolism means that a shrew can eat up to two times its body weight. It is able to get so much food because its excellent reflexes and highly fibrous muscles help it catch even the fastest insects.

Etruscan shrew

WHAT KIND OF ANIMALS ARE BATS?

Bats, of which there are more than 1,300 species, are the second largest group of mammals. Megabats, also known as fruit bats because of what they eat, can have a wingspan of about five feet. The flying fox is the largest bat. The smaller microbats are mostly carnivorous. They eat insects, and even small amphibians. Vampire bats are the only microbats that feed on animal blood.

Vampire bat

WHAT ARE RODENTS?

Rats, mice, and guinea pigs are examples of common rodents. There are over 2,270 species of rodents. Some rodents, such as weasels, are among the most effective of small predators because they are both strong and agile. Rodents typically have a pair of razor-sharp front teeth, or incisors, that grow continuously throughout their lives.

Guinea pigs

Rapid-FIRE ?

WHICH MAMMAL LAYS EGGS?

The duck-billed platypus.

Duck-billed platypus

WHAT IS BLUBBER?

The thick layer of fat in marine mammals such as whales.

Sperm whale

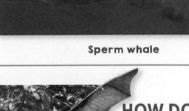

Fruit bat

HOW DO BATS FLY?

Bats have "wings" which are actually their front limbs with a membrane stretched over the fingers.

ARE BEAVERS MAMMALS?

Yes, they are mammals and, after the South American capybara, beavers are the largest of all rodents. They live in water and use their sharp teeth to gnaw through the bases of trees, felling them to dam streams. They then build their homes, which are called lodges, in the ponds created by the dams.

Beaver felling a tree

HOW BIG ARE BIG MAMMALS?

On both land and water, the largest animals are all mammals. The largest of them all, the blue whale (which can grow as long as 98 feet), lives in the water. On land, the biggest mammals are elephants. They can grow up to 13 feet in height, which is as tall as a double-decker bus, and can weigh as much as a truck. Not much smaller are rhinoceroses and hippopotamuses.

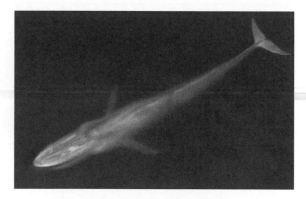

Aerial view of a blue whale

WHAT IS AMAZING ABOUT BLUE WHALES?

The blue whale, the largest known living animal on our planet, can be as large as an airplane and can weigh around 220 tons! A newborn blue whale is as big as a bus! These giants mainly feed on tiny, shrimplike sea animals called krill, which they filter out of the water in their mouths. They can eat around 4.4 tons of krill in a day!

Big?

WHAT MAKES AN ELEPHANT'S BODY SPECIAL?

A herd of African elephants

An elephant's most remarkable features are its long trunk and fanlike ears. The trunk is actually an extended, highly flexible nose that an elephant uses to pick up food, carry water to its mouth, greet other elephants, pick up heavy objects, and lots of other things. The ears, which are covered with blood vessels, help it keep cool. Elephants also have two giant teeth called tusks, which they use for digging or for defense.

WHICH IS THE **TALLEST LAND MAMMAL?**

At almost 20 feet in height, it is the giraffe. Almost half of the animal's total standing height is the length of its neck. Its legs, which can be almost 6.5 feet long, contribute to most of the rest. Its height allows the giraffe to feed on the top layer of leaves on trees that other herbivores cannot reach.

Giraffes

Hippopotamus

HOW MANY **TOES DO UNGULATES HAVE?**

The hooves of a horse

Ungulates are animals whose toenails have evolved into hooves. The number of toes they have can be either odd or even. Cattle, deer, and hippopotamuses are all even-toed. Horses belong to the odd-toed group, as do rhinoceroses.

WHAT ARE **TAKIN?**

Takin look a bit like large goats but are actually related to sheep. Takin have short horns and a stocky body, covered with dense brown hair. They live just below the tree line, high in the mountains of the eastern Himalayas and in China.

Takin

Rapid-FIRE **?**

WHAT IS THE AVERAGE WEIGHT OF THE **AFRICAN WHITE RHINO?**

Around 3.9 tons—much more than twice the weight of a mid-sized car!

African white rhino

HOW MANY **KNOWN HORSE BREEDS ARE THERE?**

Over 300.

HOW MUCH **CAN AN ELEPHANT EAT?**

About 124 lbs of food a day—the amount eaten by more than 100 people.

WHAT ARE PRIMATES?

Humans, apes, monkeys, and lemurs all belong to a group of animals called primates. They have large brains, hands that can form a good grip, and a tendency to walk on two legs.

Rapid-FIRE?

WHICH **MONKEY CAN SHOUT THE LOUDEST?**

The howler monkey's voice can carry for almost two miles!

Howler monkey

CAN **MONKEYS LIVE IN COLD PLACES?**

Yes, the rhesus macaque of the Himalayas and the Japanese macaque can survive freezing winters.

Rhesus macaque

Japanese macaque

HOW MANY KINDS OF **MONKEYS ARE THERE?**

About 260 species.

DO **CHIMPS HUNT PREY?**

Yes. Although fruit is their main food, they hunt down young animals, including monkeys.

Chimpanzee

WHY DO **MONKEYS HAVE LONG TAILS?**

To help them balance and control their movement as they leap from branch to branch. The tails of some South American monkeys are like a fifth limb with special muscles, which help them tightly grip branches.

WHAT ARE OLD WORLD AND NEW WORLD MONKEYS?

Old World monkeys, such as the baboon, live in the warmer parts of Africa and Asia. They tend to be larger than the New World monkeys. Their tails are not prehensile, which means it cannot grip objects. New World monkeys live in Central and South American forests. Many, such as the spider monkey, have prehensile tails that help them climb and hang from branches, keeping their legs and arms free to hold food.

Old World baboon / Spider monkey from New World forests

WHAT ARE LEMURS?

Lemurs

Lemurs are nocturnal animals with big, bulging eyes. They live in forests on the islands of Madagascar, off the east coast of Africa. They have soft, thick fur and bushy tails with which they scare other animals. They even use their tails to signal to other lemurs, and wave their scent around from a gland in their bottoms.

WHICH ARE THE BIGGEST AND THE SMALLEST MONKEYS?

The mandrill is the largest monkey. It can grow to about three feet tall. It lives in the tropical rainforests of Central Africa. The smallest monkey is the pygmy marmoset of the South American rainforests. It is only about 5.5 inches long (plus the tail), and weighs only between three to five oz—the weight of an orange!

Pygmy marmoset

Mandrill

Big? WHAT ARE APES?

Apes are so closely related to humans that some zoologists divide them into three kinds: great apes, lesser apes, and us humans! Great apes are almost human shaped, though they tend to have longer arms, big, protruding jaws, and are covered in fur. Gorillas are the biggest of the apes, while chimpanzees are man's closest relative and the smartest of the apes. They can communicate with varied vocal sounds, gestures, and facial expressions. Lesser apes include gibbons and monkeys. They are agile apes that live in Southeast Asian forests, and can swing swiftly from branch to branch.

Gorilla

WHAT ARE BIG CATS?

Lions, tigers, jaguars, pumas, and leopards are different kinds of big cats found all over the world (except Australasia). Though big cats differ in size from pet cats, they all belong to the same family and share many characteristics. All are expert hunters, sneaking up on their prey and then pouncing on it. Their sharp claws, powerful jaws, and fangs are deadly weapons.

Leopard

Big?

WHY ARE TIGERS SO FASCINATING?

Tiger

Tigers are the largest of the big cats in the wild, with a body longer than a tall adult human's, long tails, and black stripes on an orange-brown coat. Tigers are beautiful animals with black stripes on an orange-brown coat. The stripes help break up their outline and make it hard for prey to see them. They are solitary creatures, living alone most of their lives. Tigers hunt mostly at night, preying on large animals like deer, buffaloes, and antelopes.

WHERE DO SNOW LEOPARDS LIVE?

Their home is high in the mountains of Central Asia, all the way from the Himalayas to Russia and Mongolia. They have a beautiful, light, gray-white coat with dark rosettes, which has made them the target of fur poachers. Their favorite prey is bharel, which they stalk up steep mountainsides with ease.

Snow leopard

HOW DO LIONS HUNT?

Lions live in prides of anywhere between three to 30 animals. The females, usually all related, stay with the pride for life. Male lions usually leave when they get to about two-years old. It is the females that select and stalk the prey, then make the short dash to pounce and kill it. It is the biggest male, however, who will eat first.

A lioness attacks a buffalo

WHICH IS THE BIGGEST CAT IN THE SOUTH AMERICAN FORESTS?

The jaguar—the third largest of the big cats, after the tiger and lion. They look a lot like leopards but have bulkier bodies. The rosettes on their coats are also larger, and have a spot in the center. Unlike most cats, jaguars do not avoid water and will catch fish, turtles, and caimans, as well as deer, capybara, and other land animals.

Jaguar

Rapid-FIRE ?

ARE LIONS FOUND ONLY IN AFRICA?

No. They are also found in Gujarat, in India.

A pair of Asiatic lions

WHICH IS THE FASTEST CAT?

The cheetah. It is also the fastest land animal.

Cheetah

HOW DO TIGERS MARK THEIR TERRITORY?

They leave urine and scratch marks on trees.

WHAT IS COMMON TO MOST BEARS?

Bears are found all over the world except in Antarctica and Australia. Generally speaking, all bears have a large body, a short tail, small, rounded ears, a long, pointed snout, stocky legs with large paws, and very sharp claws. Bears are hunters and eat meat, but they also eat leaves, fruits, and nuts, which is why they are considered omnivores.

American brown bear

Big? IS THE GIANT PANDA A BEAR?

Panda

For years experts argued about whether the giant panda should be grouped with bears, with raccoons, or classified in a family of its own. Scientific study now suggests that the panda is definitely a member of the bear family. The giant panda is a rare animal that is found only in the mountainous forests of central China, where it feeds on a certain kind of bamboo tree. As the bamboo is not very nutritious, the panda spends 10-12 hours a day eating.

HOW BIG IS A BEAR CUB AT BIRTH?

Although adult bears can be very large, cubs are tiny when they are born. A huge polar bear, weighing more than 300 pounds, will give birth to cubs weighing about half a pound—far smaller even than human babies! Baby pandas weigh as little as three ounces. Bear cubs do, however, gain weight and grow very rapidly.

Mother bear with twin cubs

WHAT IS THE **MOST COMMON SPECIES OF BEAR?**

Brown bears. They are found in Europe, Asia and North America—where they are called grizzlies. Mostly solitary animals, brown bears are good hunters, able to run at speeds of up to 30 miles per hour; they also swim well.

Brown bear

CAN **POLAR BEARS SWIM?**

They are excellent swimmers and spend long periods in the freezing Arctic water. A dense layer of underfur insulates them while the longer outer coat prevents water from reaching the undercoat and skin. A thick layer of fat under the skin gives more protection.

Polar bear in water

Rapid-FIRE ?

WHY WERE **AMERICAN BROWN BEARS CALLED GRIZZLIES?**

Their fur appears to be white tipped, giving them a grizzled look.

Grizzly bear

WHICH IS THE **SMALLEST BEAR?**

The sun bear of the Southeast Asian rainforest.

Malaysian sun bear

WHICH IS THE LARGEST BEAR?

The Alaskan Kodiak bear.

Alaskan Kodiac bear

DO BEARS **SLEEP THROUGH THE WINTER?**

Brown bears, polar bears, and black bears that live in the far north sleep for much of the winter, when food supplies are scarce. But before the bears hide away in warm dens, they eat as much food as they can and put on a lot of weight. They do not go into true hibernation but sleep fitfully, living off their own fat reserves.

Bear feeding on salmon

WHAT DOES THE WORD "CANID" MEAN?

It comes from the Latin word *canis*, meaning "dog." Canids, or canines, include dogs, wolves, foxes, coyotes, dingos, and jackals—members of the dog family are found all over the world. They are meat eaters, with long snouts, long legs for chasing prey, and erect, pointed ears. They are excellent hunters, with sharp claws and strong teeth, but are also willing to scavenge. Canids were the first animals to be domesticated (tamed by people).

Rapid-FIRE?

AT WHAT AGE DO **RED FOX CUBS** BECOME INDEPENDENT?

At about eight to ten months old.

Fox cubs hiding inside a hollow log

HOW MANY SPECIES DOES THE CANID FAMILY HAVE?

About 35 known species.

HOW BIG IS A **WOLF PACK'S** TERRITORY?

About 620 square miles.

ARE **DINGOS DOGS?**

Dingos are Australian wild dogs and are generally believed to have descended from dogs introduced to the continent 5,000–8,000 years ago by ocean travelers. While they did hunt kangaroos and wallabies, today they prey mainly on sheep, rabbits, and small rodents.

Australian dingo

HOW BIG IS A **WOLF PACK?**

In areas where there are plenty of large animals for them to hunt, a wolf pack may have up to 30 wolves. Hunting in a pack means that the wolves can kill prey much larger than themselves, such as moose. Every pack has a territory, which it defends against other wolves.

A wolf pack

Wild dogs surround a buffalo and her newborn calf in southern Africa.

WHAT IS INTERESTING ABOUT THE ARCTIC FOX?

The normally brownish-gray Arctic fox changes the color of its coat to a pure white in winter. Some say this camouflages it better in the icy winters of the Arctic, others believe that the lack of melanin, or natural skin coloring, leaves hollow spaces in the hairs that trap air and provide much-needed warmth.

Arctic fox in its winter coat

ARE COYOTES SIMILAR TO WOLVES?

Native to North America, coyotes look similar to the wolf and are sometimes called prairie wolves. They are smaller, however, with longer ears and a narrow muzzle. They are mostly nocturnal hunters of small mammals such as hares, but a coyote can take down an adult deer and coyotes also hunt in packs.

A pack of coyotes

Big? HOW ARE FOXES AND JACKALS DIFFERENT?

African black-backed jackal   **Red fox**

Both foxes and jackals are small-to-medium-sized canids with pointed ears, a bushy tail, and narrow snouts, though generally jackals are a little larger and heavier than foxes. Clever hunters that prowl at night, alone, in pairs, or as a pack, they hunt small mammals, but will also eat fruit and berries and even go through trash bins in human settlements. Jackals, if hunting in a pack, have been known to kill antelopes and sheep. They live in Africa and Asia only. Foxes are found in North America, Europe, North Africa, and Asia.